Yeti

YETI

Abominable Snowman of the Himalayas

Elaine Landau

The Millbrook Press ❑ Brookfield, Connecticut
Mysteries of Science

Library of Congress Cataloging-in-Publication Data

Landau, Elaine.
Yeti, abominable snowman of the Himalayas / by Elaine Landau.
p.   cm. — (Mysteries of Science)
Includes bibliographical references (p.   ) and index.
Summary: Introduces the yeti or Abominable Snowman of the
Himalayas, recounts sightings throughout history, and considers the
reliability of the evidence advanced as proof of its existence.
ISBN 1-56294-349-9 (lib. bdg.)
1. Yeti—Juvenile literature. [1. Yeti. 2. Monsters.]
I. Title. II. Series: Landau, Elaine. Mysteries of Science.
QL89.2.Y4L365 1993
001.9′44—dc20   92-35147 CIP AC

Published by The Millbrook Press
2 Old New Milford Road, Brookfield, Connecticut 06804

For Nora Ehrman

Contents

ANNE CANEVARI GREEN

A Creature in the Himalayas

A long time ago, children growing up in the
Asian countries of Tibet and Nepal heard
scary tales of large, hairy, humanlike
beasts. According to the tales, these beasts
lived in the mountains dividing the countries,
the **Himalayas.** The creatures, known as Yetis,
were said to come after boys and girls who
disobeyed their parents. No one would want to
be captured by a Yeti. It was tall, powerful,
and had feet that pointed backward.

The Himalayas are the highest
mountain range in the world.

Few children, it was said, could escape a Yeti's clutches. Children were told that their only chance of getting away from one was to run down a steep hill. As the Yeti chased after them, its long hair would fly forward and cover its face. If the Yeti was unable to see through the tangled mass over its eyes, its young **prey** might quickly flee to safety.

Rather than risk such a frightful experience, children were encouraged to behave. And Yeti stories often proved useful to parents who wanted them to do just that.

Of course, such Yeti tales aren't true. They are very much like the monster and werewolf stories common in other parts of the world. Everyone knows that large, hairy, hunched creatures called Yetis don't track through Himalayan snowdrifts.

Or do they? Is it possible that the creatures in these folktales were based on real animals that remain unknown to science?

Demons and Strange Footprints ❏ Brian Houghton Hodgson, a British expert on the Asian religion Buddhism, published one of the first Yeti accounts. Hodgson hired some local hunters to search the Himalayas for unusual animals. In 1832 the hunters returned from a trip frightened—and empty-handed. The men said they had been scared off by a *raksha,* or **demon,** living high in the mountains. The demon they described was a furry, two-legged, mountain wild man.

*A Tibetan priest portrays a strange
creature said to haunt the mountains.*

Some think the local hunters might have come face-to-face with a Yeti. Hodgson, however, was annoyed at the men for not killing or at least capturing the creature and later concluded that they probably only saw some type of large animal.

In 1889, Major L. A. Waddell, a British officer in the Indian Medical Corps, went on a Himalayan hunting trip accompanied by native guides and local porters, who carried supplies and equipment. When they reached an altitude of 17,000 feet (5,185 meters), Waddell spotted some **footprints** in the snow. Although the tracks looked like a person's, they seemed too large to have been made by a person. Waddell didn't know who or what had made the prints. His porters quickly informed him that they were Yeti tracks. However, neither Waddell nor anyone in his hunting party had actually seen the creature walking through the snow.

Could the tracks have been made by a Yeti? Were the massive footprints familiar to local men who had spent their lives assisting hunters on Himalayan outings and seen the strange creature before? Waddell wasn't sure of the answer. Guides and porters frequently claimed that any unusual footprints were the Yeti's. Supposedly, they were anxious to please foreign hunters hoping to catch a glimpse of the mysterious animal. Major Waddell believed the tracks he had found could have belonged to a large snow bear.

❑ ❑ ❑

More than 25 years after Waddell located the strange tracks, a British forestry officer living in Tibet, J.R.P. Gent, told of another extraordinary set of footprints found in the same region. These prints were nearly 24 inches (61 centimeters) long and 6 inches (15 centimeters) wide. Gent did not actually see the footprints, but heard about them from a local resident. Some believed the creature or individual that made them was one of the *Jungli-admi*.

Jungli-admi were not Yetis. They were said to be **primitive** people living in mountain forests and foothills who were often looked down on and poorly treated by others. However, the footprints of such people would not be oversized. Therefore, some thought that the huge footprints Gent spoke of might instead be a Yeti's.

A Big Question Mark ❏ During the late nineteenth century, British and Indian hunters gave detailed accounts of the Himalayas' geography and plant and animal life. Although they described a vast variety of Himalayan animals, none of them ever mentioned a Yeti or anything like it.

Did this mean that Yetis did not exist in the Himalayas? Some people think these hunters may have camped in parts of the vast mountain range uninhabited by Yetis. Or had hunters seen such creatures and said nothing? Reporting a massive, humanlike animal might have caused a respected hunter to be ridiculed. Still others feel the Yeti wasn't seen because it doesn't exist. The Yeti's existence was a big question mark.

Have people mistaken the tracks of the Himalayan black bear, shown here, for Yeti tracks?

Information on the Yeti of the Himalayas consisted of little more than second-hand stories up to the mid-1920s. Many who heard these stories believed Yetis were still folktale characters, even though local people claimed to have seen them in various parts of the mountains. The problem was that when questioned, many of these locals admitted it was not they but someone else who had actually seen the creature and told them about it.

The Yeti had not yet captured the public's attention in Europe and the United States. But in a few years, its name would become a household word.

The Mountain Climbers' Era

Interest in the Yeti increased after
mountain climbers began to scale some of
the Himalayas' highest and most dangerous
peaks. In 1921, British Lieutenant-Colonel
C. K. Howard-Bury led a group of mountain
climbers up **Mt. Everest,** the tallest
mountain in the world. The **expedition**'s
goal was not to search for the Yeti
but to survey the area's **terrain**.

The view from the top of Mt. Everest, known as "the roof of the world."

When the climbers reached an altitude of about 21,000 feet (6,405 meters), they saw some puzzling footprints in the snow. Along the way they had identified rabbit and fox tracks. But these footprints seemed nearly human and did not appear to have been made by anyone or anything wearing shoes. How was it possible for a barefoot human to climb the rugged, snowy peak?

The climbers, like most foreigners who had seen the unexplainable tracks, were not sure what to think. But the native porters accompanying the climbers thought the tracks belonged to a "Wild Man of the Snows." This term was later incorrectly translated into English as **Abominable Snowman**—a name sometimes used for the Yeti.

A Yeti Sighting ❑Four years later, in 1925, N. A. Tombazi, a respected British photographer and member of the Royal Geographical Society, thought he might have actually glimpsed Yeti while in the Himalayas. At 15,000 feet (4,575 meters), Tombazi saw the outline of what looked like a human form about 300 yards (274 meters) from his campsite.

The sun's bright glare on the snow made it difficult for the photographer to see clearly. But when Tombazi moved closer he saw a manlike beast that walked upright. As it waded through the snow, the creature occasionally stooped to pull leaves from a bush.

Within minutes it disappeared behind some shrubs. The creature's appearance had been so unexpected that Tombazi did not have time to reach for his camera or even use his binoculars to get a closer look at it.

Tombazi later examined the area where he had seen the creature. He found five-toed footprints measuring about 6 inches (15 centimeters) long and 4 inches (10 centimeters) across. Although the prints looked somewhat human, the heels seemed to narrow to a point. Tombazi counted 15 footprints before shrubbery made it impossible to further follow the creature.

Tombazi might have actually seen bear tracks. Bear feet narrow at the heel and could match the size of the tracks he spotted. Yet the photographer felt that the prints he saw that day had a distinctly human quality to them.

Rescue by a Yeti ❏ During the 1930s a number of other supposed Yeti encounters were reported. In 1938 an intriguing Yeti account came from a European man and former military officer known as Captain d'Auvergne. According to the account, d'Auvergne was traveling alone in the mountains when he injured himself. Unable to summon help, he thought he might freeze to death as the temperature began to drop.

Just when he had almost given up hope, d'Auvergne claimed, he was rescued by a 9-foot-tall (274-centimeter) Yeti. He said the creature carried him for several miles to Yeti's cave. There shelter and warmth ensured the man's survival. Captain d'Auvergne added that the Yeti cared for him—providing food and protection while he recovered.

Once the Captain regained his health, the Yeti released him. He returned home to publish an article describing his Himalayan adventure. In his article d'Auvergne reconsidered his experience. He said he believed the Yeti who had rescued him was actually a human being. He felt that such individuals probably descended from primitive tribes of people who had remained isolated in the mountains for centuries.

D'Auvergne thought that these cave-dwelling people had adapted to the extreme cold and acquired some animal-like characteristics. Although there have been reports of "primitive" people living in Tibetan mountain caves at altitudes of 10,000 to 20,000 feet (3,050 to 6,100 meters), there is no positive proof of their existence. But if such people do exist, could they have been mistaken for Yetis?

Many found the Captain's story unbelievable. They dismissed the Yeti as the product of overactive imaginations or publicity seekers.

Side-by-Side Footprints ❏In the 1950s, a string of new sightings caused some people to renew their belief in the existence of Yetis. One mountain climber found two sets of tracks in the snow that appeared to have been made by large human feet in boots. The climber thought that the footprints belonged to a team of German mountain climbers who he thought were in the area. However, he later learned that the Germans had not climbed the slope after all.

Is the cave-dwelling creature depicted here a Yeti or one of the "primitive people" d'Auvergne claimed he saw?

Once again the tracks seemed more human than animal. It was also unlikely that they had been left by other, unknown climbers. The footprints suggested two people walking side by side. Climbers almost always walk through deep snow in single file. They follow the leader's footsteps, thereby creating only one set of tracks. Some thought the prints might have been made by two Yetis walking together through the snow, though no one could explain their bootlike appearance.

*Climbers follow one set of tracks
up a Himalayan peak.*

Eric Shipton.

Attention-Grabbing Photos ❑ An important development in the Yeti story took place in November 1951. British climbers Eric Shipton and Michael Ward were returning from a Mt. Everest expedition. At 18,000 feet (5,490 meters), along the edge of a **glacier** between Nepal and Tibet, the two came across some fresh footprints in the snow. The tracks measured 13 inches (33 centimeters) in length. Each footprint's heel was broad, and while there were five toes, the two inner toes were longer than the rest. Shipton took some clear, well-focused photos of the tracks.

Was this Shipton photo of a Yeti print?

His pictures captured the public's attention. Many thought they proved the Yeti's existence. Reporters mobbed Shipton as he stepped off the plane in England returning from the expedition. All were anxious to interview him, but not because he had climbed the world's tallest mountain. Instead, they were eager to hear more about the mysterious footprints.

Yeti became an object of worldwide interest. Tourists were encouraged to visit the Himalayas, which now were referred to as the home of Mt. Everest *and* the Yeti. Before long Yeti-hunters from around the globe flocked there to search for this half-human beast.

An Era of Expeditions

During the 1950s a number of large-scale Yeti-searches were launched. Participants in a 1954 expedition organized by the British newspaper the *Daily Mail* discovered some footprints and a scalp that might have belonged to a Yeti. No definite conclusions could be drawn from their findings, however.

In 1957, Tom Slick, a Texas oil millionaire, financed a mission to search for the Yeti. Known as the Slick-Johnson expedition, this hunt yielded photographs of unexplained foot-prints. Also found were frozen body parts thought to belong to a Yeti. But these turned out to be the paw of a snow leopard and a human hand.

*Members of the Slick-Johnson
expedition watch for a Yeti, prepared
with a rifle to hunt it down.*

Although these expeditions failed to capture a Yeti, reports told of a zoo in Tibet exhibiting a large Yeti. *The Daily Telegraph,* a British newspaper, published a story telling how a man named Parekli, an Indian mountain climber, had seen the captured creature. He described it as short, covered with rust-colored hair, and having a long, cone-shaped head. The article caused much excitement, but Parekli's story was never confirmed.

For years American and European explorers searched for the Yeti without success, even as Yeti sightings by Tibetans grew more common. A priest at a mountain monastery described how a Yeti approached their place of prayer during a winter storm. According to the priest, the creature was about 5 feet (152 centimeters) tall and covered with silvery gray hair. It walked out on two legs from behind some bushes, though at times it bent over to scamper on all fours. Before leaving, the Yeti grunted, scratched itself, and played with a handful of snow.

More False Evidence ❏ Though no one ever managed to produce a living or dead Yeti, its skeleton, or outer skin, another search effort, known as the Himalayan Scientific and Mountaineering Expedition, was organized in 1960–1961. A New Zealand mountaineer who had climbed to the top of Mt. Everest in 1953, Edmund Hillary, led the expedition. It set out to achieve several goals. In addition to hunting Yetis, its researchers hoped to learn more about glaciers and how mountain climbers adapted to high altitudes.

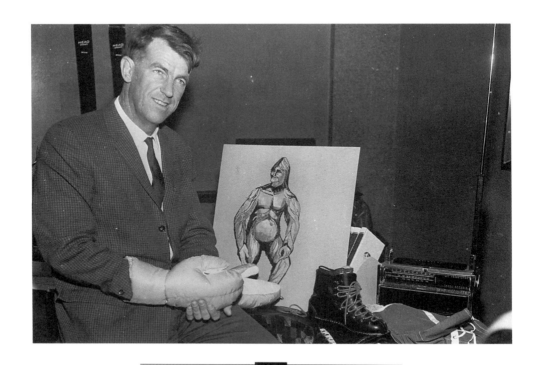

*Edmund Hillary with his mountain
climbing gear and a drawing of a Yeti
before the Himalayan Scientific and
Mountaineering Expedition.*

The expedition's work was thorough—and extremely discouraging for Yeti believers. After examining what was supposedly a Yeti skin discovered in the snow near a mountain village, the researchers found it belonged to a blue bear. Since the blue bear is somewhat rare, local residents hadn't readily recognized the skin and had concluded it was a Yeti's.

The researchers also obtained a so-called Yeti scalp, which they were told was over 240 years old. The Tibetan villagers who had given it to them regarded it as a sacred object and had used it in religious dance festivals. But when scientists examined the scalp in a laboratory, it proved to belong to a rare Himalayan goat-antelope.

A member of Hillary's expedition holds the scalp that was obtained.

Following the expedition, interest in Yeti declined. Fewer mountain climbers investigated unusual tracks they found in the snow, and scientists no longer reacted enthusiastically to newly announced Yeti developments. Reporters found other stories to cover.

Nighttime Sightings ❏ But just when it seemed that the Yeti might be almost forgotten, news of a British expedition led by the highly respected mountain climber Don Whillans reached the public. In March 1970, Whillans came across some footprints of a kind that he had never seen before, 13,000 feet (3,965 meters) up in the Himalayas. He photographed the tracks, which, like previously discovered prints, seemed neither human nor animal.

Later that night Whillans caught a glimpse of a large apelike creature crossing a distant ridge. Had this same animal made the tracks he had found earlier? These and other questions regarding the sightings remain unanswered.

In 1972 a Tibetan on an American expedition spotted what he thought might have been a Yeti wading in a nearby stream one night. When he shone his flashlight in the creature's face, it quickly turned and ran. The following morning other expedition members found tracks they couldn't identify in the area of the sighting.

Whillans photographed these tracks, believing them to be a Yeti's.

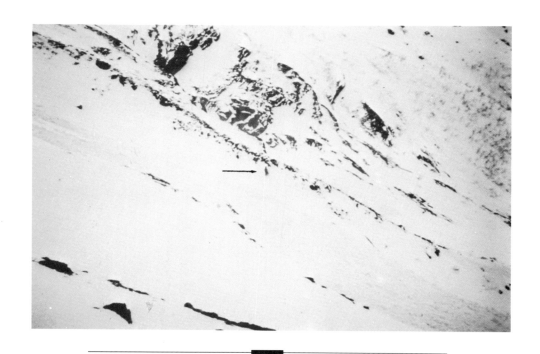

The arrow in this photo points to what Wooldridge
believed was a strange Himalayan creature.

Wooldridge's Photograph ❏Then in 1986 what seemed one of
the most convincing reported Yeti encounters occurred. A
British long-distance runner named Anthony Wooldridge did
a solo run in the Himalayas to raise money for charity. While
in northern India near Nepal, at an altitude of 11,000 feet (3,355
meters), Wooldridge came across a strange set of footprints.
He followed the tracks to a large shrub.

There behind the leaves was a tall creature with a large,

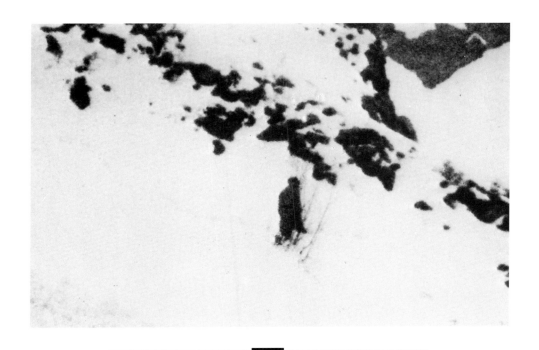

Wooldridge thought the creature, shown here
close up, was a Yeti standing in the snow.

square head. Its body appeared covered with dark hair, though its upper arms had less hair than the rest of its body. Standing on two feet, with its legs spread slightly apart, the creature gazed down the snowy mountain slope.

Wooldridge took out his small camera to capture the humanlike beast on film. But because the runner didn't have the correct lens for long-range shots, the photo was unclear. As a result, it was difficult to plainly see the creature's features.

Nevertheless many felt the form in the photograph was definitely something they had never seen before.

Their hopes were dashed the following year. In the summer of 1987, Wooldridge returned to where he thought he had seen the Yeti. But with the snow melted, he realized that he had only photographed a large, unusually shaped rock.

An Unsolved Mystery

Descriptions of Yetis have varied to such a degree that some people speculate that, if Yetis do exist, there may be different types of them. In fact, Tibetans have spoken of both a very large Yeti, known as the *Dzu-teh,* and a shorter one, called the *Meh-teh.*

The *Dzu-teh* is said to stand about 8 feet (20 centimeters) tall and have extremely long, thick body hair. The *Dzu-teh* supposedly kills and eats cattle. It also tends to react violently if approached by humans.

The *Meh-teh* is a smaller and perhaps less frightening Yeti. Like the *Dzu-teh,* it is also said to eat meat but preys on smaller animals. The *Meh-teh* reportedly lives in rocky mountain cliffs below the **snow line.** Although this Yeti is often compared to an ape, part of its name—*Me* (Meh)—means man. In naming this unusual creature, Tibetans noted its likeness to a human being.

Both types of Yetis supposedly make sounds. While the *Dzu-teh* seems to roar, the *Meh-teh* is said to make a loud, catlike cry and to whistle shrilly.

Continuing Controversies ❏ While debates go on over whether there are two varieties of Yetis, controversies also continue to surround footprints and reports of sightings. Those who dispute sightings argue that, since these creatures were often seen from a distance or after dark, witnesses could have mistaken a large bear or some other animal for a Yeti. Many also feel that at least some reports have been false or very exaggerated.

Researchers have even found a scientific explanation for some of the oversized footprints discovered in the Himalayas. When the sun shines on tracks in snow, the snow melts, making the tracks appear much larger than they actually are. In some cases, two animal tracks have even blended together to look like one tremendous footprint.

Cryptozoology ❏ Nevertheless, some trained scientists suggest that the Yeti may be real. Many of these scientists are cryptozoologists. **Cryptozoology,** a fairly new science, is the study of hidden or unknown animals.

Cryptozoologists stress that although some footprints thought to be Yeti's may have become enlarged when the snow melted, others were sighted right after its reported appearance and could not have become larger in this way.

These scientists also argue that some now-familiar animals were once completely unknown to us. For example, inhabitants of the African country of Rwanda described a dark, hairy, humanlike beast. Scientists in the United States and Europe never took these reports seriously, figuring that such an animal could not be real. But in 1901, when German Captain Oscar Von Beringe returned from Africa with a skin from one of the creatures, they were forced to change their minds. Von Beringe had discovered a gorilla, an animal previously unknown to Rwanda.

From the 1850s to the early 1900s explorers journeyed to different parts of the world to find once unknown animals such as the pygmy hippopotamus, the Komodo dragon, and the giant panda. Early reports of the existence of these creatures had been laughed at as well.

In 1938 a South African fisherman made one of the most interesting discoveries of an unknown animal when he pulled a strange-looking fish out of a river. No one recognized the fish, and it was eventually given to a team of scientists to examine. The scientists soon realized that they had previously seen only **fossils** of the fish. It was a **coelacanth**—a **species** thought to have been **extinct** for at least 60 million years.

*Discoveries of cryptozoology:
(facing page) A pygmy
hippopotamus with its baby.
A Komodo dragon (above).
A coelacanth (right).*

Cryptozoologists and Yeti-believers feel that if a fish thought to be extinct by the scientific world was finally caught in a river, then the Yeti may exist as well. Some cryptozoologists think that the Yeti may even be some unknown kind of ground-dwelling ape that adapted to the cold.

Could Yetis possibly be a small population of these oversized apes that somehow escaped extinction? This theory has yet to be proven. But believers insist that with thousands of square miles of unexplored territory in the Himalayas, it's impossible to definitely say that there's no such thing as the Yeti. The mystery remains unsolved.

Glossary

Abominable Snowman—English term for Yeti, incorrectly translated from a Tibetan term meaning "wild man of the snow."

altitude—height above sea level.

coelacanth—kind of fish once thought to be extinct.

cryptozoology—the science of hidden or unknown animals.

demon—evil spirit or devil.

Dzu-teh—type of Yeti about 8 feet (244 centimeters) tall.

expedition—journey to a remote area for a purpose such as exploration.

extinct—term describing a plant or animal that no longer exists.

footprint—impression left on a surface by a foot.

fossil—impression of an animal or plant from an earlier age preserved in rock.

glacier—large body of ice moving slowly down a slope.

Himalayas—large mountain range in central Asia.

Jungli-admi—Tibetan term for primitive, mountain-dwelling people.

Meh-teh—type of Yeti shorter than the *Dzu-teh*.

Mt. Everest—world's highest mountain, measuring 29,028 feet (8,854 meters) high.

prey—animals hunted as food by other animals.

primitive—term meaning undeveloped or belonging to an earlier age.

raksha—Tibetan term for a mountain-dwelling demon.

snow line—place on a mountain where dry land ends and snow-covered land begins.

species—biological term for a grouping of related animals or plants that are capable of reproducing (breeding) with each other.

terrain—land area.

Further Reading

Antonopulos, Barbara. *The Abominable Snowman*. Milwaukee, Wisconsin: Raintree Publications, 1983.

Facklam, Margery. *And Then There Was One: The Mysteries of Extinction*. Boston: Little Brown, 1990.

Gelman, Rita Golden. *Monkeys and Apes of the World*. New York: Franklin Watts, 1990.

The Geography Department. *Nepal in Pictures*. Chicago: Lerner Publications, 1989.

Lasky, Kathryn. *Traces of Life: The Origins of Human Kind*. New York: Morrow, 1990.

Parker, Steve. *Mammal*. New York: Alfred A. Knopf, 1989.

Pringle, Laurence P. *Bearman: Exploring the World of Brown Bears*. New York: Scribner's, 1989.

Salsam, Millicent E., and Joyce Hunt. *A First Look at Animals That Eat Other Animals*. New York: Walker, 1990.

Wilkinson, Paul, ed. *Early Humans*. New York: Alfred A. Knopf, 1989.

Index

Page numbers in *italics* refer to illustrations.

About the Author

Elaine Landau received her Bachelor's degree
from New York University in English and
Journalism and her Master's degree in Library
and Information Science from Pratt Institute.
She has worked as a newspaper reporter, editor,
and youth services librarian, and has especially
enjoyed writing over 50 books for young people.